Bully for

illustrated by **Toni Goffe**

It is easy to be a bully.

You just have to make people do what you want ...

Child's Play (International) Ltd

Swindon   **Bologna**   **New York**
© M. Twinn 1991   ISBN 0-85953-355-7 (soft cover)   Printed in Singapore
ISBN 0-85953-365-4 (hard cover)
Library of Congress Catalogue Number 91-9891

HOW TO BE A BULLY

You can have
all sorts of FUN ...

Calling names ...

Anything will do, as long as you say it nastily:
Fatty, Skinny, Shorty, Baby ...

Mimicking ...

Torturing …

Hitting …

… Anything that will make them cry.

Make them give you things.

Make them let you play with their things.

Make them do things they are frightened to do.

Make them do things YOU are frightened to do.

Make them do things they don't want to do.

Make them look silly.

Make them do wrong things.

Make them bully others.

BE CAREFUL!

Be careful!

Pick someone smaller.
Pick someone younger.

Start with kids
who are new in town,
who don't have friends.

Especially, if they are 'different'.
Maybe they look different or talk differently.

Make sure they are weaker, too!
Make sure they don't have someone to defend them.

Make sure they won't run and tell!

Threaten them with what will happen if they do!
"Telling tales is not playing the game."

You can often bully people who are bigger and older.
Even some teachers.

They won't want anyone
to know they can't handle the class.

Often, the class will back you up,
because it's the teachers against you.

LEADER OF THE GANG

You don't have to be big to be a bully.

Be clever!

Find others to do your work!

Look for big ones!

Choose younger ones,
or less clever ones,
who will look up to you.

Now you are leader of the gang!

You will have to keep them in line.

Sometimes, praise them.
Sometimes, let them share the spoils ... and the fun.

That may come in handy, if one of your victims complains about you.

If you choose stupid enough people,
they will keep on trying to please you
and to earn your approval.

They will try to look like you and dress like you.

IF YOU ARE CAUGHT

What do you do if you are caught?

You can say:

"He started it.
Ask the others ..."

"The others started it ..."

"It was only a game ..."

Do anything to save your skin.

Even cry.

"I didn't realise …
I won't do it again."

BEING A BULLY IS NOT ALL FUN

It is not all fun being a bully.

It is NOT fun for *them* ...

Nobody likes you ...

Not even most of your gang.
They are just scared of you.

If you are found out,
they won't stick up for you.
Everybody likes to bully a bully!

You may not like yourself.

Maybe you would prefer to have friends,
to be looked up to.

Nobody wants to be your friend.

Some people are even sorry for you ...

WHY ARE YOU A BULLY?

It's a gift to some people.
They are born bullies.

Maybe, they learned that crying
got them attention when they were babies.
Children who always get their own way at home
sometimes become bullies, when they don't
get their own way at school.

Sometimes, it's the opposite.

Some brothers and sisters
and even parents are bullies.

Children who are bullied at home
often learn that bullying is the only way
to get what they want.

Bullies are almost always weak.

But sometimes,
if nobody stands up to them,
they achieve positions of power.

They really do think that they are superior
and that other people should do what they say.
They call bullying 'leadership'.

They surround themselves with bullies
and yes-men.

National leaders who are bullies cheat the people.
They may start wars.

Often, they are overthrown by violent enemies.

Real respect and love are hard to achieve.
Real leaders know their own weaknesses
and respect others.

They never choose to fight,
unless there is no other way,
or unless they are confronted
by a bully.

Then they show courage
and resolution
and fight to the end.

We all bully sometimes,
to get what we want.

BULLYING IS JUST BEING SELFISH.